Copyright © 2025 by Educate Learners

Published by Educate Learners

All rights reserved. No part of this publication may be reproduced, distributed, or transmitted in any form or by any means, including photocopying, recording, or other electronic or mechanical methods, without the prior written permission of the publisher, except in the case of brief quotations embodied in critical reviews and certain other noncommercial uses permitted by copyright law.

First Printing, 2025.

ISBN: 978-1-951573-63-8

www.educatelearners.com

The opposite of

up

is

down

The opposite of

inside

is

outside

The opposite of

full

is

empty

The opposite of

dirty

is

clean

The opposite of

morning

is

night

The opposite of

awake

is

asleep

The opposite of

young

is

old

The opposite of

big

is

small

The opposite of

front

is

back

Thank you for reading!

Get a free year long subscription to our online education resource library when you purchase any one of our books.

Code: EDBOOKS

educatelearners.com

www.ingramcontent.com/pod-product-compliance
Lightning Source LLC
Chambersburg PA
CBHW041603070526
44586CB00003BA/68